The Blue Wife Poems

The Blue Wife Poems

by

Hayley Mitchell Haugen

Cover image by Shay Culligan
Cover art by BCGraphix

ISBN: 978-1-63980-178-7

Kelsay Books
502 South 1040 East, A-119
American Fork, Utah 84003
Kelsaybooks.com

for the blue

Acknowledgments

Poems in this collection have appeared previously in the following journals:

Anti-Heroin Chic: "While I Was Sleeping"
Gyroscope: "Would You Please Stop Whistling, Please?"
I Thought I Heard A Cardinal Sing ~ Ohio's Appalachian Voices: "The Blue Wife"
Misfit Magazine: "Get the Bitch a Lobotomy"
Nerve Cowboy: "Blue Wife Imagines Her House Is Burning"
Poetry Pacific: "The Blue Wife"
The Red Ogre Review—Primeval Monster: "Night Terrors"
The Women Inc.: "Blue Wife Adopts Puppies, "Blue Wife puts too much stock in a good day"
Writing in a Woman's Voice: "0 Days of Yes"

I'd like to thank those who have been instrumental in helping me complete this little book. Research and sabbatical funding for this project was generously supplied by Ohio University. Sandy Coomer at The Rockvale Writers' Colony provided a quiet and welcoming retreat where I wrote the first drafts of these poems during two residencies. Matthew Wolfe understands the emotional truth behind these poems all too well and freely gave his friendship and support as I navigated their landscapes. "Therapy Steve" Tackett offered a safe space in which to speak about difficult memories. My friends in poetry: Wilma Stanley Acree, George Franklin, Kari Gunter-Seymour, Susanna Connelly Holstein, Sean Kelbley, Stephanie Kendrick, David B. Prather, and Sherrell Wigal critiqued work in progress and guided my revisions. Finally, my mother, Delia Gurge, always my first reader, said, "Yes. You need to write these poems."

Contents

Contents

"Call a woman crazy and she'll justify your faith."
—Nancy Mairs

"Or if thy mistress some rich anger shows,
Emprison her soft hand, and let her rave,
And feed deep, deep upon her peerless eyes."
—John Keats

The Blue Wife

read a story once about a woman
who walked into a cornfield, just left
her gaping husband at a roadside Super-Quick
and strolled into the embrace of night,
the fireflies closing the gaps behind her,
briefly lighting the spaces she had been.

Blue Wife, though, is no romantic: the forest
behind her house slowly encroaches,
all coyote howl and jawbone, deer tick
and smothering kudzu. Poison ivy strangles
her shrubbery, darkens the sun porch walls,
and the hope that is the firefly, is too fleeting
to light the way.

Black Dogs & Blue Words

"As metaphor and analogy become the only tools with which to understand depression, the rhetoric becomes the reality of experience—both for sufferers, who come to understand their *selves* through the language of illness, and for researchers, who have access to the illness only through that language."

—Kimberly K. Emmons, *Black Dogs & Blue Words*

You are falling into the abyss /
over the edge / heavy / weighed down /
carrying a load / slowed down /
down in the dumps / sinking /
falling / hitting rock bottom /
in the basement / in a real dark night
of the soul / in the bottom of a well /
outside the self / a blank slate /
on the wrong path, a rough road /
in uncharted territory / lost /
under a cloud, a shadow / in a fog /
isolated / locked inside the mind /
imprisoned / running out of gas /
empty / stuck / malfunctioning /
running from the black dog / battling
the beast, your dragons / at war
with yourself. Try to get back on track /
cross that bridge / lift your spirits /
pick yourself up / recharge / find the door
to your psyche / unburden yourself /
find balance / don't surrender /
fight back, fight harder / win the battle,
march out of the dark / weed the garden,
cultivate / look on the bright side.

Get the Bitch a Lobotomy

for Alice Hood Hammatt, the first US pre-frontal lobotomy patient

She was "a master at bitching and really led her husband a dog's life."
—Walter Freeman

Freeman took Alice from Alice
in 1936, severing her neural connections
to relieve her from depression, her restlessness,
to relieve her husband from her bitching,
her anxious garrulousness. After,
she was calm, in that wax dummy kind of way
the history books would chronicle,
the activists would question.
Perhaps she felt some loss of dignity,
fell into a childlike stubbornness and sloppy eating,
or maybe, like a thousand others to come,
she sat inert, disoriented to time, to place, to self,
as she tried to recall some feeling she once had,
some talent, but why worry about what is normal:
Every patient probably loses something
by the operation, some spontaneity, some sparkle,
some flavor of the personality.

Blue Wife is a dog who's learned her own helplessness,

curled tight into the couch cushions again
like a bitch caged—an electrified home—
no use attempting to avoid her pain.

Prozac, sunshine, wheat bread offer small gains,
but with every peak, a new gorge to roam,
curling tight into the couch cushions again.

Nothing she's tried prevents the shocks' keen aim—
might as well gnaw on her own tired bones,
no use attempting to avoid her pain.

Sleeping mid-day, she's missed her chance to win
back some small moment of joy, and alone,
she's curled tight into the couch cushions again.

Housework is a pulse she can't maintain—
the beds unmade, the dishes left undone;
no use attempting to avoid her pain.

If she could shower, dress, walk in the rain,
she might advance, might not be the one
curled tight into the couch cushions again,
with no use for attempting to avoid her pain.

Blue Wife discovers the Symptom List

in her new issue of *Home & Garden:* What's the difference,
she reads, between a bad case of the blues and depression?
Take the Quiz—What sounds familiar?

Do you feel like you're failing as a wife, a mother,
like even the dogs go unnoticed for days?
Are you convinced that you are an imposter,
that your students know you are faking it,
that you can't hide anxiety behind a smile?

Do you visit your friends and fidget
in their comfortable armchairs?
Do you attend conferences only to sneak off
to Bob Evans to eat an omelet on your own?
This condition, this loss of pleasure is known
as anhedonia. It is cause for concern.

Does your husband say, *Are you sleeping again?*
Do you have trouble with waking in the night,
wondering if you've left the garage open, if you paid
the lawn guy, if your mother, too, is awake
at this late hour worrying, worrying, worrying?

Did you join Weight Watchers and eat that Quarter Pounder
anyway? Did you count the Points for the half bag of Oreos?
How many times did you reread that line in that poem?
How many words float daily out the open door?
How did you miscalculate your son's tuition?

Are you irritable and angry?
Do you curse when you burn the dinner?
Do you honk the horn?

Do you throw things? Are you impatient
with grocery clerks and automated banking?
Do your kids ask, *Why are you screaming?*

Are you still enraged at the uncle who molested you
forty years ago? Do you fume over the family
who allowed their shame to shield him?

When the looming semi-truck speeds towards you
on Industrial Parkway, do you imagine yourself swerving
into the no pass zone? When the Ohio River is running high
and fast, do you picture yourself swirling among its debris?

How did you score? Seek a counselor, a psychiatrist,
be sure to share this list if these symptoms sound familiar,
if you think you might be suffering from depression,
if you are a woman.

Blue Wife puts too much stock in a good day

when she welcomes that tinge of happiness
that enfolds her when working—a cool breeze
along her edges, lifting her mood in small measures,
like the Ecuadorian butterfly tapping its way
across lavender at the conservatory show.
Suddenly clear-headed and light and just *happy,*
despite the gray day, the rain, she texts her friends,
her mother, swears she's eaten her way back
to good health—no sweets, no white breads,
the extra pounds starting to shed—or maybe
the doTERRA oils diffusing in her workspace
with *Endurance* and *Hope,* like it's always been
as easy as just plugging in and misting two years
of dark humors away. But the next day,
the very damned next day, that feeling is gone—
as quickly as it descended. The dogs too needy,
the kids too loud, the afternoon nap like a Siren call,
and then, those two hours wasted, the headache worse,
the mind scattered, unfocused, as though taken by surprise,
like when that yellow butterfly snapped closed its wings
and revealed a shock of blue.

Dear Valium

dear Executive Excedrin,
dear Mother's Little Helper,
you beckoned us out
of the age of anxiety
and we listened,
followed the worried-well,
the functioning class,
straight out of suburbia,
left our recording studios,
and film sets, our churches,
to land and languish
in the Valley of the Dolls.
We thought we could trust you,
in this "whole new world,"
but instead, we lost ourselves:
Marilyn, Liz, and Tammy Faye
all falling by the wayside
while you kept moving on,
right into the mainstream.

0 Days of Yes

The healthy living app asks, again,
if I drank water before breakfast,
but I hear: Did you take out the trash?
Did you grade those papers?
Did you change the kids' sheets?
Did you call the Dr. about that stomach thing?
Did you write that poem?
Did you save any money this month?
Did you throw out the expired salmon?
Did you email that student back?
Did you go to the gym like you said you would?
Did you take in the clothes donations?
Did you read your friend's book?
Did you use that expensive new eye cream?
Did you paint that spot on the wall?
Did you text your mom?
Did you eat less?
Did you trim the guinea pig?
Did you send that card?
Did you love your husband?
Did you sweep the porch?
Did you scrub the tub?
Did you support your girlfriend?
Did you check your kids' grades before the new term?
Did you finally make the cookies with the mint chips?
Did you remember to shower?
Did you think of anyone except yourself?
Did you try harder?
Did you make amends?
Did you spend your time wisely?
Did you do even one thing to make a difference?
Did you ever?
Did you?

—for Sherrell Wigal

Blue Wife in the kitchen

only threw meat that one time
when the burgers burnt so badly
their black edges crumbled,
as gritty as tile grout. The smoke

alarm wailing, the toddler screeching,
she smashed the blue Fiestaware
on the countertop, sent those
over-grilled bastards rolling

across the stove. "God damn cooking,"
she cried, hurtling a charred disc
past her husband's quiet shudder
in the dining room. She crumpled,

then, amongst the weight
of her ordinary domesticity:
the meal planning, the grocery shopping,
the cooking, the cleaning.

I hate those *women,* she thought,
the ones who make it look so easy,
who adore their Instant Pots and pin
recipes to their browser tabs, the ones

who don't wilt a little every time
a child asks, "What's for dinner?"
Her woes spilled over like last week's
chili as the sun set beyond her kitchen

curtains. She hoped her family
might offer some comfort, a release
from her anxiety, but she knew
they looked on and saw only

her foolishness, knew
she would still have to feed them.

"In depression, the lights are off, but somebody's definitely home.
She just can't make it to the door to let you in."
—Martha Manning

Blue Wife lights the NO VACANCY sign

when she loses her womb to adhesions:
two caesarians, the gallbladder mess,

creating a sticky web of scarring.
And now, there simply is no room

for desire, for mothering, no nourishing space
inside herself to welcome wayward travelers,

her friends. Left behind like two forgotten suitcases,
her ovaries ache sometimes, reminding her

of places she's been, but the blue estrogen pills
hold her just this side of nostalgia,

keep menopause at bay. She is neither
too hot, nor too cold. No anger

no weeping, yet her rhythms are in flux,
despite what the doctors say. Forgetful,

she makes half a bed, eats half a sandwich,
drifts midway through her son's homework

assignment, her mind wandering
some stark hallway, pondering renovations,

like choosing wallpaper. What could emerge
from this blank space? She can't see it.

She's done with decisions,
just done managing it all.

—for Donna Hilbert

Blue Wife imagines her house is burning,

how she stands by, waits to call the fire dept.
Goodbye, she waves, to her husband's collections,
as 5,000 movies melt frame by frame.
CDs crackle in their unwrapped cellophane,
vintage posters curl behind museum-quality glass.
Thirty years of vinyl warps and bends.

Here, she thinks are all the family vacations
we never had, the roof repairs. How many
flaming board games—their plastic markers
reduced to toxic rainbow-colored puddles—
would it take to buy 21st century windows,
to fix the sunroom, paint the front porch?

How much has to burn before this space
feels like her own, before she is no longer
smothered?

How to Come off Prozac

Try not to think of this as withdrawal,
but rather, discontinuation syndrome:
fatigue is nothing to be concerned about,
the nausea, insomnia, muscle pain.
You might feel agitated, irritable.
The world is returning: do not be startled
should you have profoundly vivid dreams.
Dizziness, blurred vision, tingling, sweating—
in four to six weeks these will dissipate.
You are returning to the person
you were: you might feel *everything*.

Blue Wife Offers Some Suggestions

For God's sake, encourage me to shower,
see me, know that I am slipping
before I'm fully gone. By now,
can't you see when I'm struggling?
Do I have to tell you *every* time,
point out the signs? When I explode
when the kids ask *what's for dinner,*
that's a sign. Don't expect dinner.
The dishes? Do them. When I weep
over charred burgers, when I throw things,
when I haven't monitored our kids'
homework for weeks, when I haven't noticed
the kids at all, when I'm mindless,
playing a video game for hours, this is not
how I prefer to spend my time.
When I ignore the dogs, don't open mail,
forget to switch the washing to the dryer,
this is when you should just check *in*.
Don't say, *Are you napping again?*
Don't suggest, *maybe some exercise will help.*
Don't tell me to *choose* to be *happy,*
to go do something *fun*. Know
that there is no easy win for us here,
that I'm not asking you to fix me.

Blue Wife dresses up for the Vampire Circus,

wears blue jeans and black lace, her best boots with stiletto heels.
A pro wielding the flatiron, applying her eyeliner without a hitch,

she adds lip gloss with a bit of sparkle. And it's not *for* anybody,
just a night out with a girlfriend. The Romanian troupe

makes an effort as well, their sequined leotards shooting
off stars in the stage lights. The acrobats wow the rural crowd

with their strength—handstands on a partner's shoulder,
limber contortions through hoops of fire. The aerialists dance,

suspended by thin wires above the stage; a knife thrower
looks like Jason Momoa. But underneath the atmospheric music,

elaborately painted stage props, dry-ice seeping from crypt
and demon lair, Blue Wife senses something adrift in the script.

The impresario is aging out, forgetting his lines. Vampire clowns
are not funny, just ridiculous. Preying on an audience member,

bringing them on stage, the shtick goes on too long, breaks
the fourth wall irreparably. Blue Wife leaves depleted, exhausted

with showmanship. She doesn't shower for thirteen days.
The Vampire Circus moves on to the next small town.

Blue Wife buys extra deodorant. Somewhere in Iowa,
a circus performer misses a beat, drops a plate, slips grasp

of the trapeze and falls from the sky. Blue Wife thinks another day
of dry shampoo will suffice—wonders if anyone will notice.

Blue Wife adopts puppies

and walks them to feel the weight of her own self
lifting; in the morning, after the rain, the droplets
echo leaf to leaf in her forest-ringed suburbia;

the pups investigate deer droppings, parade
the street triumphantly gumming tree limbs,
two drooling mouths to one end each, wobbling

shoulder to shoulder, their big heads and little paws
performing a balancing act of pure wonder
for an audience of one. At night, she counts

the insomniacs, their TVs glowing long past sunset,
the bats zipping overhead, the puppies curious to know
all cats and leaf crinkles; they scuffle over earthworms

and crabapples, reminding her—no matter what—to see
the littlest details of each long day: velvet ears,
black rubber noses, exuberant, tail-thumping love.

The Career of Depression

after sociologist David Allen Karp

1. Assessing

Our culture says dis-ease is a disease,
that normalcy is health, conformity;
we brush away our pain when we agree
our discomfort is a pathology.
At this inchoate stage we have no words
to label bewilderment *depression*
and work instead on goals to move towards,
a change in circumstance, our aggression.
A situation's left behind, perhaps
the days will smoothly soften, rub less raw,
but there's an innate sense of true collapse;
we know something is wrong, we just feel flawed:
    a mooring's slipped with body, mind, and self—
    a consciousness kept on a private shelf.

A consciousness kept on a private shelf,
I was afraid to let my family know
I'd lost my grip on what was mental health,
but couldn't name what made me feel so low.
My days stretched out, each hour needing filled
with me not knowing what I'd done before;
a heart that raced, a mind that needed stilled,
I was a house without an open door.
Somewhere inside a woman roamed alone;
with time, I thought, I would surely find her.
I didn't know that she was simply gone,
didn't know the stranger in the mirror:
    then suddenly I saw that she was me,
    the first veiled glimpse of new identity.

2. Redefining

The first veiled glimpse of new identity
reveals itself full-on when we decide
to move away from *something's wrong with me*
to, most fiercely, *I know I'm sick inside.*
Our problems, then, have moved beyond control,
lives in turmoil, crisis situations,
until we go to doctors to unfold
a diagnosis, a clear conception.
In therapy there's stigma and there's hope,
just disavow the labels and move on;
others tiptoe around you—let them cope—
you're not obliged to teach them your new song.
    Move forward with a plan, a faith in will,
    in science, as you swallow that first pill.

With faith in science, I swallow that pill,
wash it down with a swig of come-what-may;
my therapist, though, seems a little girl,
too young, I'm sure, to stand what I might say.
No ring, no kids, no failings of her own,
I find it hard to share my dark secrets,
feel badly when I have to let her go
but leave her platitudes with no regrets.
I wait, instead, for pills to make me whole,
awaking to a foggy kind of dream
where I don't give a damn what illness stole;
I'm neither euphoric nor sad, it seems,
    existing now in Zoloft's blank slate bliss—
    enough myself to know there's more than this.

3. Reinterpreting

Enough ourselves to know there's more than this,
we come to grips with illness as a thing;
a search for answers, some clue we have missed,
helps reinterpret what each new day brings.
There must be darkness lurking in our past,
a specter that's been waiting to emerge,
reminding us the good we've known can't last
unless we work to rid it, make the purge
of all that holds us down, what keeps us back,
of all that misevaluates our worth;
a theory forms for what we've lost—or lack—
a path reveals itself; we venture forth.
    With eyes on what we feel will set us free,
    the journey makes us find new ways to be.

The journey's made me find new ways to be,
but first I had to face what made the hole,
embrace the damaged child, to let her see
the pain others had dealt had taken toll.
I scrutinized my marriage, sensed a loss
of love I'm sure had long ago been there,
I calculate what my leaving would cost,
wonder if I am even being fair.
The kitchen screams for paint in a panic,
so too the redo of the downstairs room:
busyness—or is it more like manic,
to throw oneself to projects done too soon?
    There's no one magic cure, no simple balm
    to capture peace, regain a space of calm.

To capture peace, regain a space of calm,
I open mornings as a special gift;
the journey's made me find fresh ways to warm
to what I have to offer, what I give.
Enough myself, more healthy now than ill,
my future holds a different form of me;
a faith in healing, I take one last pill,
the first veiled glimpse of new identity.
I'm careful to protect what I became
but take consciousness from that private shelf;
I won't let others push me to feel shame:
accept me *now,* you must accept my self.
     I'm done, I think, trying so hard to please
     in culture where dis-ease is a disease.

The Deep Ends

After a few weeks, I tell Therapy Steve that I am ready to share my story. *Jumping into the deep end,* he says, with no idea of where I'm about to take him. My story starts in a pool, in the deep end, I say, in the arms of an uncle teaching me to swim.

> Water so blue-clear
> I wonder how no one saw
> under the surface.

While I Was Sleeping

I did not hear Kathryn crying, six doors down
in her flannel nightdress, cold and confused,
calling for help from her dewy backyard,
her silver walker shining by the watchful eye
of the moon. Long before the medics came,
I had already closed my windows, checked
for strangers behind my shower curtain, retired
behind the locked door of my room, and laid there,
dreaming. Two nights later, the police came,
flashlights illuminating the pain of our houses.
They called for Sheila, across the street
with her beautiful, dark-stained garage door
and trellis roses. *Come out,* they said, *don't do it.*
I woke up then and wished those police would poke
their nightsticks into the deepest closets of all our houses,
that they would upturn beds and dusty bookcases
and accuse all the sick and crazed and suicidal
among us, cleansing our homes each by each
until they found him, in that corner house just
out of sight of my own, the man I called uncle,
the man who molested me, my fifth-grade friend,
twenty years' worth of little cousins since then,
while I feigned safety, while I feigned comfort,
while I was sleeping.

Night Terrors

The President is taking Hydroxychloroquine,
tweeting, "I started taking it because I think it's good.
I've heard a lot of good stories." Has he heard the ones

about side effects? we wonder: agitation, hallucinations,
paranoia, and psychosis. And don't forget the night terrors,
my mother says, don't you remember? And I do,

and I don't. I had never connected my midnight
tossing, the startled wakefulness, the screams
rushing my parents to my room, to the generic,

Plaquenil, I was taking in my twenties, not for Covid,
but for lupus, the wolf howling deep inside my bones.
I had simply thought I remained body-haunted,

was having my "dark-man" dreams, was lost, again,
in the grip of my childhood tormentor who lived, still,
just blocks away, unaccused, unmolested.

I was that young girl framed in my mother's hallway,
all dark circles and seriousness in my patchwork sundress.
I was seven, eight, nine . . . and barely sleeping,

not concentrating, falling behind. Things had happened to me
for which I had no words. At night I revisited them
in dreams. Forty years later, the president takes a pill,

and a door opens upon my earliest memory—
an image I've always had with me but never knew
where to file. This is a day-terror, perhaps hallucination:

I am swinging in the garden, my mother inside,
doing mother-things, when I see him, a grown man
with a dark wolf's face, on the other side of the brick wall

where the local lizard suns himself, the wall where the people
are supposed to stay on the outside.
Suddenly, my heart is pounding. Urine runs down my legs.

I can't stop the swing fast enough, thinking, *please, please
don't open the gate*. That night I awake in twisted sheets,
tangled in the first "dark-man" dream.

Listen. I am not twenty, or nine or seven.
I am hardly anybody.
I am three.

Will You Please Stop Whistling, Please?

My dad is genetically programmed
to whistle "Hey Jude." I hear him
washing the cars of my childhood,
always humming, whistling, no weight
of the world upon his shoulders.
Even now, at age eighty, he hoists
a paint-roller with the ease of a tune,
replasters the bathroom tile, patches
a hole in the neighbor's roof,
whistling his way, making it better.
It's that other whistler who haunts me—
my uncle, whistling over each Thanksgiving
turkey, half-naked in his kitchen,
sweat rolling down his huge,
impossibly pregnant-looking belly.
Even on holidays, he wore nothing
but swim shorts. Outside, he allowed
his fat penis to loll obscenely outside
his gaping trunks. I didn't know
exhibitionist, knew only his whistle,
the beautiful, terrible sound
of that perfect pitch. Neil Diamond,
Roger Whitaker, Cat Stevens—
he whistled whatever the family danced
to. Each time his fingers entered me,
his quiet niece, a child, he whistled.
Some days now, I am blindsided.
My husband's weak whistle, I think,
is hardly worth the effort, but when
he hits a note just right, my skin crawls.

I want to ask him, Will you please stop
whistling, please? But I don't want to be
that woman, that damaged girl, that one
person at the party who can't appreciate
a little music.

House of Sun

There was no shame in this house, my childhood home
passed through cousins' hands and back to mine again.
When I return, I find thick green stalks of something
growing in the backyard—four so purposefully placed
they cannot be weeds.

Its secrets deep under layers of paint, the dust of generations,
this house was protection. Here, no leering eyes
of the man called neighbor, uncle, grandfather, the same
fat man to all of us—the same pool—the same thick fingers
searching the folds of our skin—the same chaise lounge
and unfamiliar male genitals.

This house was silent, and now it's singing. Some child
has spoken, and the dust motes stir in the darkest closets
of memory, while outside the flowers are blooming
high above the fence post: first one heavy face opens,
then two and four, and others are waiting, careful,
but deliberate, lifting towards the sun.

What the Hands Know

When asked what people need to be happy,
Freud responded, *Lieben und arbeiten—love and work.*

The happiest people rely on their hands,
digging deep into good, moist earth, working
the vegetable patch, the flower garden, moving
through the seasons from seed to table. The pleasure
is in the effort, its own purposeful reward,
the intentional connection a kind of healing.

Think of the mother's touch that heals,
the swaddled infant in nurturing hands,
the acts of grooming, a child rewarded
by the warm washcloth, the gentle work
of untangling unruly hair, the pleasure
of cool fingertips as a fever moves

across the brow. Even patients who moved
through the asylums were heart-healed
by supporting their own sustenance, pleased
by the abundant tasks for their restless hands,
making shoes, repairing mattresses, working
as tailors, seamstresses, broom-makers, rewards

reaped through constant motion, rewards
displayed in handmade bird cages, canaries moving
in every shop space, filling each full workday
with song. The craftswoman, too, shapes healing
through the steady exertion of her own hands—
over clay, over glass, over the unique pleasure

of the fountain pen traversing the open, pleasant
space of the empty line. I once ignored the rewards
afforded those with—I thought—clever, gifted hands,

didn't know I had only to keep mine moving,
to forego inertia for the doing, embrace the healing
motivated by the body in action working

for its own peace of mind. Focused on the work
of afghan-making, I embraced the new and pleasing
repetition of fingers guiding wool; I healed
my racing thoughts by painting canvases, rewarded
as each tiny, numbered space became a thing, moved
from idea to actuality with the help of my hand.

And through this work, in these moments, I briefly healed
myself, pleased the sorrowful aspects of my being, felt rewarded,
like moving toward freedom, unbinding one's own hands.

Works Consulted

The following works have informed my personal understanding of depression and have inspired my thinking within many of the poems in this collection.

Barber, Charles. *Comfortably Numb: How Psychiatry is Medicating a Nation*. Vintage, 2009.

Emmons, Kimberly K. *Black Dogs & Blue Words: Depression and Gender in the Age of Self Care*. Rutgers University Press, 2010.

Karp, David. *Speaking of Sadness*. Oxford UP, 2017.

Kline, Nathan S. *From Sad to Glad: Kline on Depression*. G. P. Putnam, 1974.

Lambert, Kelly. *Lifting Depression: A Neuroscientist's Hands-on Approach to Activating Your Brain's Healing Power*. Basic Books, 2008.

Manning, Martha. "The Legacy." *Unholy Ghost: Writers on Depression*. Ed. Nell Casey, Harper 2002.

The Complete Guide to Mental Health for Women. Eds. Lauren Slater, Jessica Henderson Daniel, and Amy Elizabeth Banks, Beacon, 2003.

The Mental Health of Women. Eds Marcia Guttentag, Susan Salasin, and Deborah Belle, Academic Press, 1980.

About the Author

Hayley Mitchell Haugen holds a Ph.D. in 20th Century American Literature from Ohio University and an MFA in poetry from the University of Washington. She is currently Professor of English at Ohio University Southern, where she teaches courses in composition, American literature, and creative writing. Her chapbook *What the Grimm Girl Looks Forward To* appears from Finishing Line Press (2016), and poems have appeared or are forthcoming in *Rattle, Slant, Spillway, Chiron Review, Verse Virtual,* and many other journals. *Light & Shadow, Shadow & Light* from Main Street Rag Publishing Company (2018) is her first full-length collection. She edits *Sheila-Na-Gig online* and Sheila-Na-Gig Editions.